Dogs

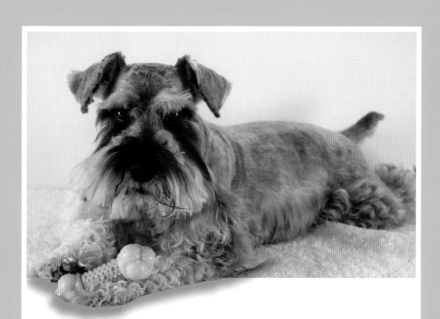

Written by Sandra Iversen

Look at this dog.
It is big.

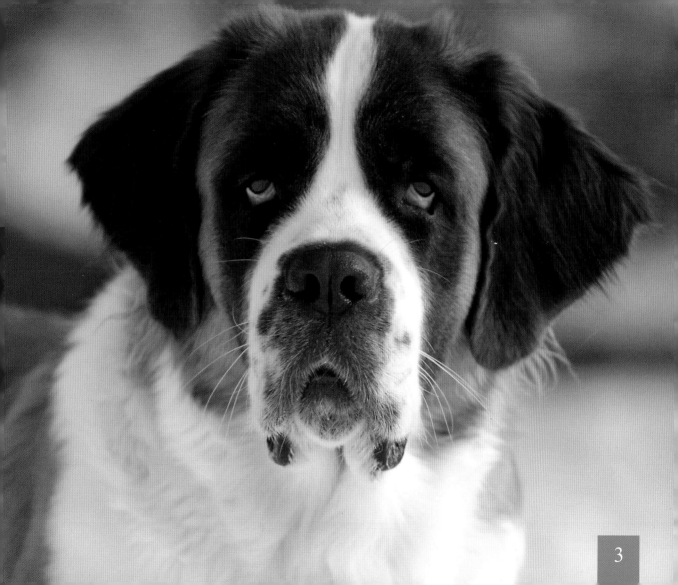

Look at this dog.
It is not big.

4

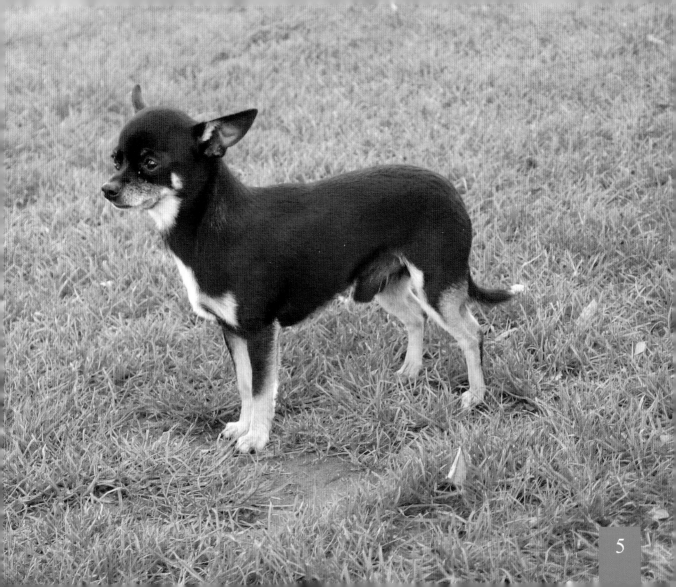

Look at this dog.
It is hot.

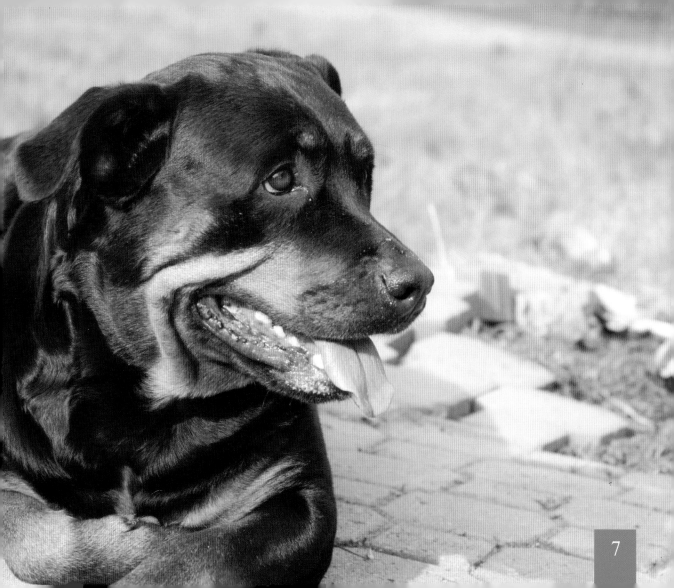

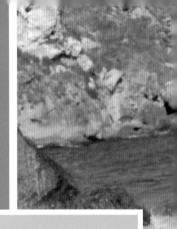

Look at this dog.
It is not hot.

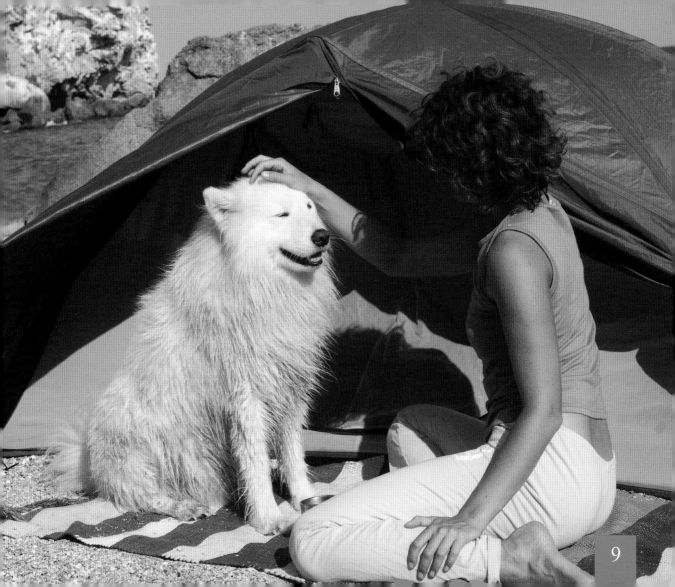

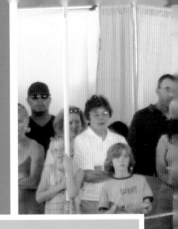

Look at this dog.
It has a job.

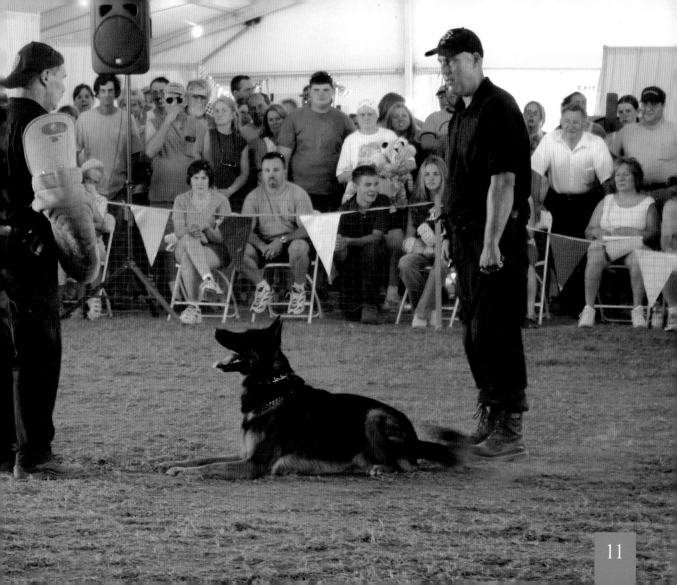

11

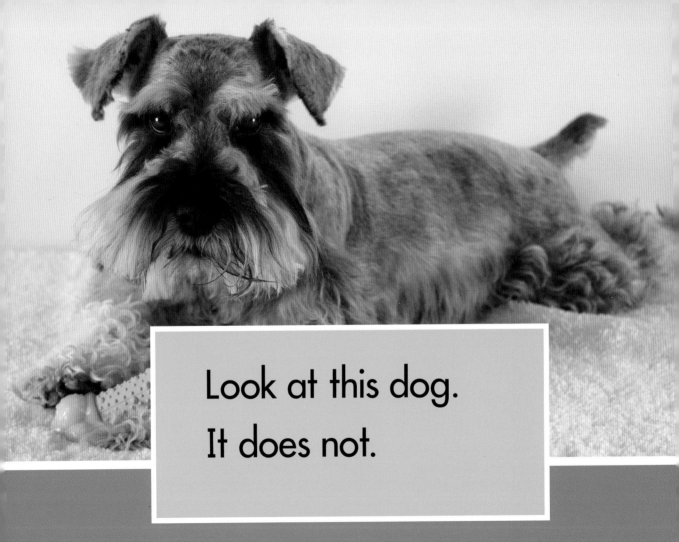

Look at this dog.
It does not.